OUR Values

RESPECTING PRIVACY

By Steffi Cavell-Clarke

CRABTREE
PUBLISHING COMPANY
WWW.CRABTREEBOOKS.COM

Published in Canada
Crabtree Publishing
616 Welland Avenue
St. Catharines, ON
L2M 5V6

Published in the United States
Crabtree Publishing
PMB 59051
350 Fifth Ave, 59th Floor
New York, NY 10118

Published by Crabtree Publishing Company in 2019

Author: Steffi Cavell-Clarke

Editors: Kirsty Holmes, Janine Deschenes

Design: Jasmine Pointer

Proofreader: Melissa Boyce

Production coordinator and prepress technician (interior): Margaret Amy Salter

Prepress technician (covers): Ken Wright

Print coordinator: Katherine Berti

Photographs

All images from Shutterstock

Printed in the U.S.A./122018/CG20181005

Library and Archives Canada Cataloguing in Publication

Cavell-Clarke, Steffi, author
     Respecting privacy / Steffi Cavell-Clarke.

(Our values)
Includes index.
Issued in print and electronic formats.
ISBN 978-0-7787-5426-8 (hardcover).--
ISBN 978-0-7787-5449-7 (softcover).--ISBN 978-1-4271-2221-6 (HTML)

    1. Children's secrets--Juvenile literature. 2. Secrecy--Juvenile literature. 3. Privacy--Juvenile literature. I. Title.

HQ784.S42C38 2018   j155.4'18   C2018-905491-3
                                  C2018-905492-1

Library of Congress Cataloging-in-Publication Data

Names: Cavell-Clarke, Steffi, author.
Title: Respecting privacy / Steffi Cavell-Clarke.
Description: New York, New York : Crabtree Publishing, 2019. |
  Series: Our values | Includes index.
Identifiers: LCCN 2018043787 (print) | LCCN 2018045851 (ebook) |
  ISBN 9781427122216 (Electronic) |
  ISBN 9780778754268 (hardcover) |
  ISBN 9780778754497 (pbk.)
Subjects: LCSH: Privacy--Juvenile literature. | Data protection--Juvenile
  literature. | Online identities--Juvenile literature.
Classification: LCC BF637.P74 (ebook) | LCC BF637.P74 C38 2019 (print) |
  DDC 155.4/1892--dc23
LC record available at https://lccn.loc.gov/2018043787

CONTENTS

Words that look like **this** can be found in the glossary on page 24.

WHAT ARE VALUES?

Values are the things that are important to you, such as **respecting** privacy or caring for the environment. People who share the same values often think or act in similar ways. This helps them work and live together in a **community**.

Helping others

Respecting the law

Sharing your ideas

Values make our communities better places to live. Think about the values in your community. What is important to you and the people around you?

Telling the truth

Caring for the environment

Working hard at school

WHAT IS PRIVACY?

Privacy means being able to keep some things to yourself. It means you can choose not to share something with others.

It is a good idea to keep some things private, like our computer passwords or our bodies. Other things should be shared with others, such as our feelings.

We all have the right to keep some things private. Knowing what you should and shouldn't keep private will help to keep you safe.

Staying safe is important. We should not keep private anything that might hurt us or others.

RESPECTING PRIVACY

To respect something is to **value** it and treat it with importance. Privacy is something that we should value and respect.

You should never keep private something that could harm yourself or others, even if someone has asked you to.

When a person trusts that you will respect their privacy, it can be upsetting for them if that trust is broken. When privacy is broken, a person might feel that you don't respect them or their wishes.

PROTECTING PRIVACY

It is important that we know how to protect our own privacy. One way we can protect our privacy is by learning about **consent**. This is when you clearly say "yes" when someone asks you to do something. If you want to keep something private, you can choose to not give consent.

There are parts of our bodies that we should always keep private. Sometimes a doctor, nurse, or family member may need to see the private parts of your body, but they should always explain why and ask you if it is okay first. Remember that you are in control of your body and you are allowed to say "no" if you feel unsafe.

SHOWING RESPECT TO OTHERS

It is very important that we respect other people's privacy. We shouldn't make people show or tell us things that they don't want to. Just like you, everyone has a right to keep things to themselves. We need to listen if a person does not choose to give consent.

Sarah and her friends get changed in separate bathrooms before they have swimming lessons at the public pool. Sarah chooses to change into her bathing suit in private. She trusts that her friends will not **disturb** her while she changes, and she does not disturb her friends when they do the same.

KEEPING SECRETS

Sometimes, you might have a secret that you want to keep private, or that someone else has asked you to keep private. Though we should listen when someone asks us to keep something private, not all secrets should be kept.

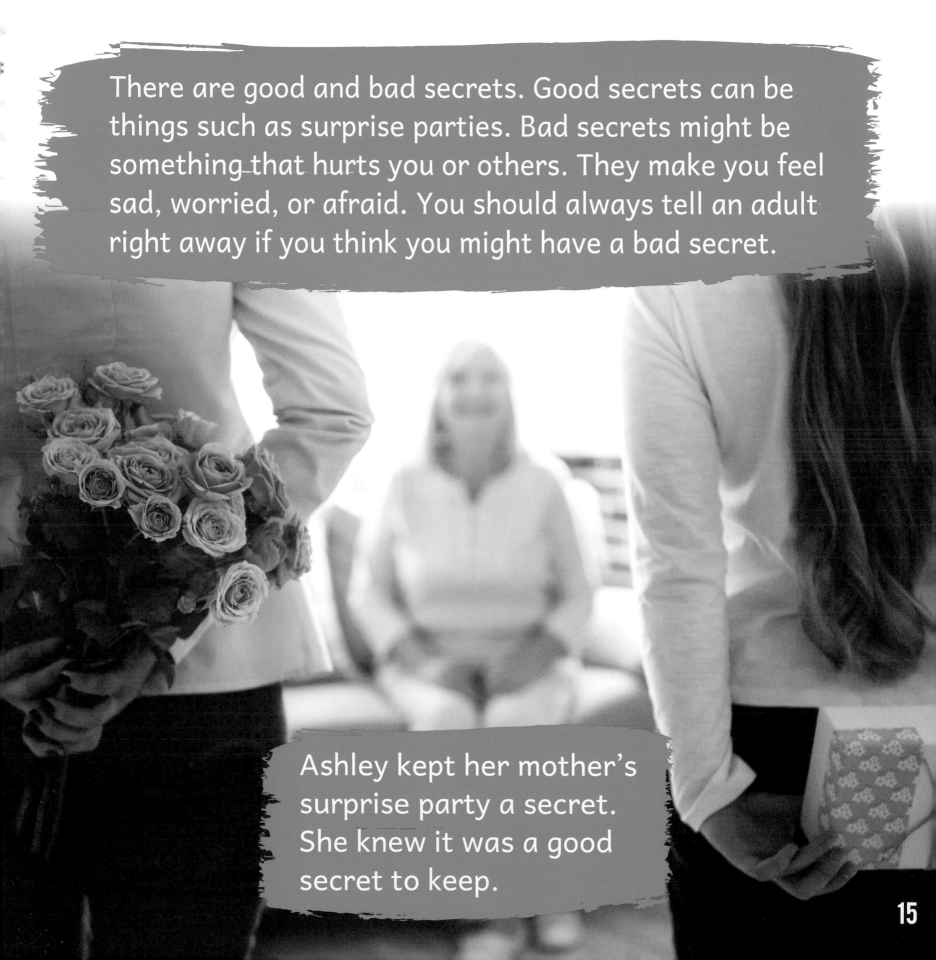

There are good and bad secrets. Good secrets can be things such as surprise parties. Bad secrets might be something that hurts you or others. They make you feel sad, worried, or afraid. You should always tell an adult right away if you think you might have a bad secret.

Ashley kept her mother's surprise party a secret. She knew it was a good secret to keep.

ASKING FOR SUPPORT

Trusted adults such as parents, caregivers, and teachers can give you advice and help you when you have a secret or some private information that makes you feel uncomfortable or unsafe. It is important that you always talk about things that make you feel worried or upset.

You always have the right to say "no," even if it is to a family member or friend. If a person tries to convince you to change your decision about your consent, they may not be someone you should trust.

Remember that your parents care for you and have your safety in mind when they ask you to do things. However, you should still talk to other trusted adults if you feel unsafe.

PRIVACY ON THE COMPUTER

One place where privacy is important is on the computer and the Internet. People often store, or keep, **personal information**, such as where they live, on their computers. It is important that personal information stays private.

You should never **post** personal information on the Internet. Personal information stored on computers should be kept safe.

Never post anything on the Internet that you wouldn't want other people to see. There are many people on the Internet that you do not know. Once something is posted online, it may become impossible to remove.

It's a good idea to use the computer only when a parent or caregiver is there, too.

PASSWORDS AND PRIVACY

Passwords are secret words that you choose, which unlock a computer. Passwords help to keep our computers **secure** and stop other people from using them.

Joseph doesn't share his password with his friends because it is private.

People use social media to **communicate** with other people from around the world. You can use social media to share information, photos, and videos with your friends and family.

Make sure that you keep your social media **accounts** private, so **strangers** cannot see what you are sharing. Do not post your personal information on social media, either.

SHOWING YOU CARE

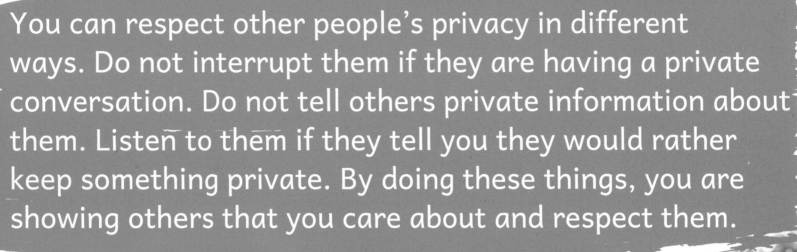

You can respect other people's privacy in different ways. Do not interrupt them if they are having a private conversation. Do not tell others private information about them. Listen to them if they tell you they would rather keep something private. By doing these things, you are showing others that you care about and respect them.

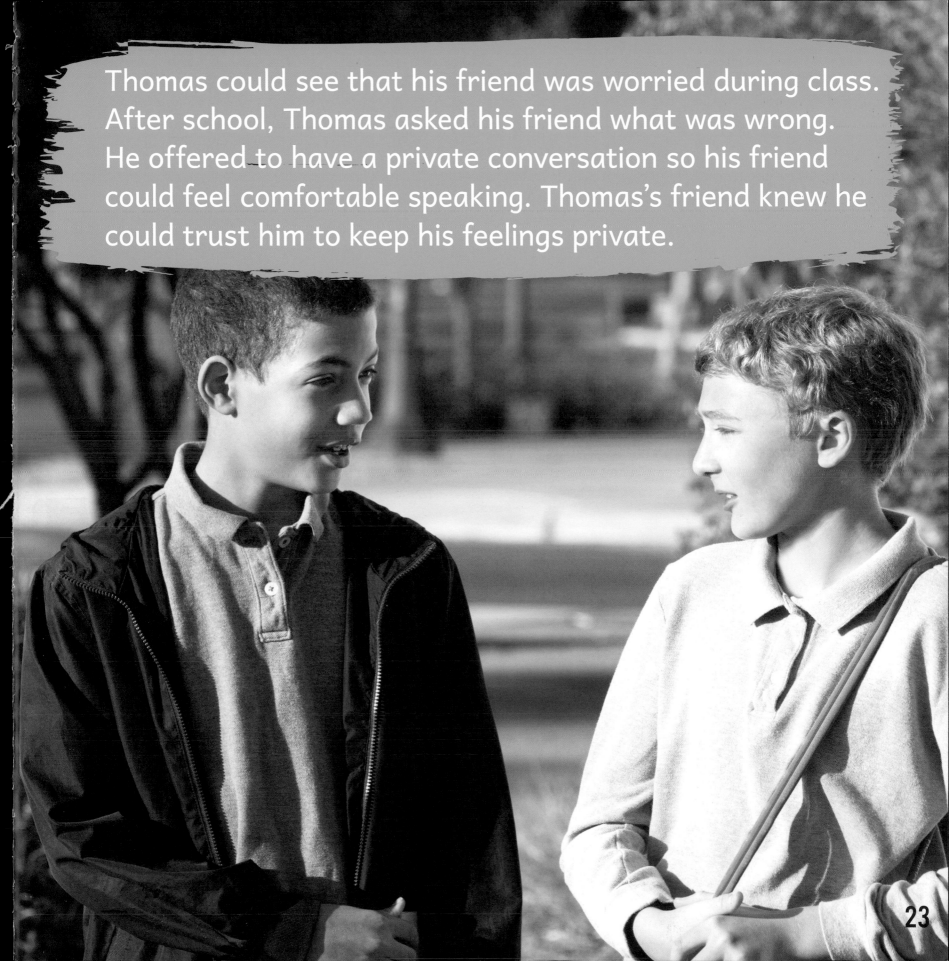

Thomas could see that his friend was worried during class. After school, Thomas asked his friend what was wrong. He offered to have a private conversation so his friend could feel comfortable speaking. Thomas's friend knew he could trust him to keep his feelings private.

GLOSSARY

accounts [*uh*-KOUNTs] Parts of a website that only you can access

communicate [k*uh*-MYOO-ni-keyt] Pass information between two or more people

community [k*uh*-MYOO-ni-tee] A group of people who live, work, and play in a place

consent [k*uh* n-sent] Agreeing to do or allow something

disturb [dih-STURB] To bother or interfere

environment [en-VAHY-*r̃uh*n-m*uh*nt] Your surroundings

law [law] Rules made by government that people must follow

personal information [PUR-s*uh*-nl in-fer-MEY-sh*uh*n] Details about you, such as your age, your name, and where you live

post [pohst] Upload something online

respecting [ri-SPEK-ting] Giving someone or something the care or attention it deserves

secure [si-KYOOR] Protected and safe

strangers [STREYN-jers] People you do not know

value [VAL-yoo] Treat something with importance

INDEX